101 Retirement Lifestyle Questions

ISBN 978-1-951915-22-3

Published by Retirement Project LLC

Created By Robert & Amie Laura
In cooperation with:

Retirement Coaches Association

Certified Professional Retirement
Coach Designation

I

Table Of Contents

Introduction

It's been said that the quality of your life is dependent on the quality of the questions you ask yourself.

As members of the Retirement Coaches Association, we feel this is particularly true for the transition from work-life to home-life, so we have assembled 101 questions to help you think about, see, and plan for retirement in a completely new light.

A perspective that focuses on you and the things that are most important to you, rather than your money and how long it may last.

The book is packed full of non-financial questions designed to help you envision everyday life in retirement.

Specific sections help segment and organize the questions. However, there are no rules or requirements to go through each section or to answer every single question, one after the other.

Feel free to hop around and focus on questions that resonate the most with you… or share one or two of your favorite questions on social media to engage family and friends in fresh retirement conversations.

As you make your way through the book, take time to notice similar themes and key words that come up multiple times.

Consider them key pieces to the retirement puzzle that you can use to connect the dots and design a more personal and intentional retirement lifestyle plan.

Section 1: The Warm Up

Questions: 1-12

Do you think we need to retire the
word retirement? Why or why not?

_____

_____

_____

_____

_____

2

What are 3 key elements for a
perfect day in retirement?

_____

_____

_____

_____

_____

3

What factors are more important than money when it comes to designing your life in retirement?

_____

_____

_____

_____

4

What have you had to sacrifice, give up, or put on hold in order to get to retirement that you would like to make up for now?

_____

_____

_____

_____

_____

5

Most people are aware of what they will gain in retirement like time and freedom, but what things will you lose or need to replace?

_____

_____

_____

_____

_____

6

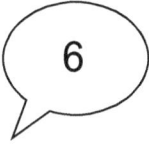

How will you introduce yourself in retirement without mentioning your former work or career life?

_____

_____

_____

_____

_____

(7)

What are three ways in which
you will know that you are thriving
and not just surviving in retirement?

_____

_____

_____

_____

_____

8

What are two non-financial reasons that might cause struggles or even failure in retirement?

_____

_____

_____

_____

_____

9

What is something you definitely
want to avoid in retirement?

_____

_____

_____

_____

10

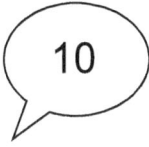

Why do you think retirement is one of the top 10 most stressful life events?

_____

_____

_____

_____

_____

11

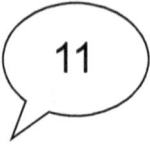

What is your existing passion,
hobby, or role that defines you
outside of your work-life?

_____

_____

_____

_____

_____

12

What's more important to your retirement: Achieving a certain lifestyle or the act of no longer doing your specific job? Why?

_____

_____

_____

_____

_____

Did You Know?

The origins of retirement can be traced back to the German chancellor Otto von Bismarck who developed the first "social insurance" program in 1889.

It was designed to appeal to the working class and to combat a growing Socialist movement.

Somewhat cynically, Bismarck set the retirement age at 65 since he knew hardly anyone lived beyond that point.

In 1935, US President Franklin D. Roosevelt proposed the Social Security Act.

Similar to Bismarck's strategy, the retirement age was set at age 65, which few people reached since average life expectancy at the time in America was only 61.7 years. (1)

Section 2: A Deeper Dive

Questions: 13-30

13

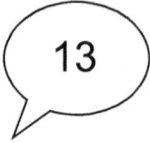

What are some of the key, non-financial factors that you think people should consider when making a retirement decision?

_____

_____

_____

_____

_____

14

Senses including hearing, vision, and taste can slow down or begin to retire at the same time people do. How might a declining sense or two impact your life in retirement?

_____

_____

_____

_____

_____

15

What does it mean to live a good life in retirement?

_____

_____

_____

_____

_____

16

What are some of the most significant world events that shaped you and your generation?

_____

_____

_____

_____

_____

17

What saying, mantra, or quote are you using, referring to, or repeating to help get yourself to or through your retirement transition?

_____

_____

_____

_____

_____

18

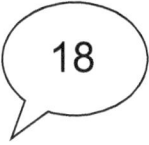

How have your priorities, values, and or beliefs shifted or become more enhanced as you've moved closer to retirement?

_____

_____

_____

_____

_____

19

Why should we keep, change,
or eliminate traditional
retirement ages?

_____

_____

_____

_____

20

What would be different if we didn't have a so-called retirement phase of life?

_____

_____

_____

_____

_____

21

What positive examples do you have of people succeeding with a retirement transition?

_____

_____

_____

_____

_____

22

What negative examples do you have of people struggling with a retirement transition?

_____

_____

_____

_____

_____

23

How much are you looking forward to the day you retire and what's one thing you're really excited about?

_____

_____

_____

_____

_____

24

How can you maintain a sense of adventure and curiosity in retirement?

_____

_____

_____

_____

_____

25

How would you describe your
overall attitude and mindset
around getting older?

_____

_____

_____

_____

_____

26

Share a positive and a negative way that you think technology may impact or play a role in your retirement?

_____

_____

_____

_____

_____

27

What aspects of your non-financial
retirement life have you written
down to help you replace your
work identity, fill your time, stay
relevant and connected, and to
keep mentally and physically active?

_____

_____

_____

_____

_____

28

What are three things you want to see, do, or accomplish in your first year of retirement?

_____

_____

_____

_____

_____

29

How might adjusting to retirement
be harder or take longer than
you think?

_____

_____

_____

_____

_____

30

If you could trade all of your retirement savings in for one thing, would you do it...and what or who would it be for?

_____

_____

_____

_____

_____

Anonymous Retirement Plan

Outside a popular Zoo there is a large parking lot for 150 cars and 20 busses. For 25 years, its parking fees were managed by a pleasant attendant. Then, one day, after more than two decades of never missing work, he didn't show up. So the zoo called the city council to ask for a replacement.

The council did some research and shared that the lot was the zoo's own responsibility. The zoo stated that he was never on their payroll and must be a city employee. But city council said that the man was never on their payroll either.

Meanwhile, in some beautiful villa is a retired man who installed a ticket machine on his own and then simply started collecting the fees. At $900 a day for 25 years, this guy made over 10 million dollars… and no one even knows his name! (2)

Section 3: Personal Life

Questions: 31-50

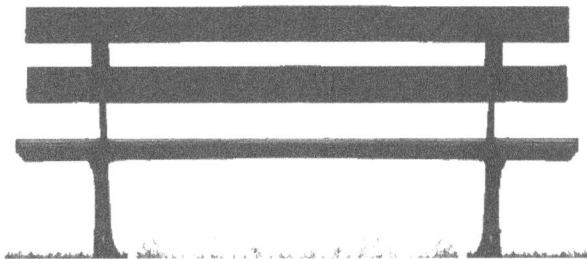

31

What are your 2 favorite topics
to discuss and which one could
you read 100 books about or
Watch 100 videos on?

_____

_____

_____

_____

_____

32

What would you do if you knew
you couldn't fail?

_____

_____

_____

_____

_____

33

What do people turn to you for
that comes easy to you?

_____

_____

_____

_____

_____

34

People who know you well
believe you are at your best
when you are…?

_____

_____

_____

_____

_____

What natural talents, skills, abilities, or resources would you like to be more intentional with in retirement?

_____

_____

_____

_____

_____

36

What is one personal life lesson that you can use to help navigate the ups and downs of retirement?

_____

_____

_____

_____

_____

37

If you could have any view from your bedroom window in retirement, where would it be and what would you see?

_____

_____

_____

_____

_____

38

What is one thing you don't want
to regret in the next:
  1 year?
  3 years?
  5 years?

_____

_____

_____

_____

_____

39

Which activities do you look forward to the most and make you feel completely in the zone?

_____

_____

_____

_____

_____

40

What is something you have never done but want to try in retirement?

_____

_____

_____

_____

41

What role will faith, spirituality, or mindfulness play in retirement?

_____

_____

_____

_____

_____

42

How do you nurture and maintain meaningful relationships?

_____

_____

_____

_____

_____

How can you ensure your life in retirement doesn't end up like a groundhog's day scenario where each day just repeats itself?

_____

_____

_____

_____

_____

44

In terms of life-long learning, share two or three topics that appeal to you and that you would like to investigate in retirement?

_____

_____

_____

_____

_____

45

How do you plan to stay motivated and inspired to pursue goals or impact others during retirement?

_____

_____

_____

_____

_____

46

What are some of the ways you find joy and fulfillment in your everyday life?

_____

_____

_____

_____

47

How do you like to express your creativity, and is there a creative art, skill, or talent you would like to develop or improve in retirement?

_____

_____

_____

_____

_____

48

Do you prefer to read, listen, watch, or experience things in order to learn and gather information... and what is something you are currently enjoying in this format?

_____

_____

_____

_____

_____

49

What assumptions or thoughts about retirement might be holding you back?

_____

_____

_____

_____

50

When do you feel most like yourself, where are you, and what are you usually doing?

_____

_____

_____

_____

_____

Retirement Humor

Strange things happen when various professionals retire:

- ☑ Golfers lose their drive
- ☑ Accountants lose their balance
- ☑ Bank managers lose interest
- ☑ Mechanics re-tire every day
- ☑ Musicians decompose
- ☑ Watchmakers wind down
- ☑ Academics lose their faculties
- ☑ Arborists branch out

When is the best time to start thinking about your retirement? *Before the boss does!*

Why did the robber retire? *He couldn't take it anymore!*

I have more jokes about retired people... *but none of them work. (3)*

Section 4: Work Life

Questions: 51-60

What is one trait, skill, or talent that you're known for at work or in your career?

_____

_____

_____

_____

52

Which people helped you the most at important crossroads in your work life and how did they play a role in shaping your life today?

_____

_____

_____

_____

_____

What work life milestones have been important to you and what helped you reach them?

_____

_____

_____

_____

_____

54

In what ways might your career or work life be similar or different than your calling?

_____

_____

_____

_____

_____

55

What are the pros and cons of having an encore career or working part-time in retirement and why or why aren't you considering them?

_____

_____

_____

_____

_____

56

What tools, skills, and experiences from your work life may be most and least helpful for you in retirement?

_____

_____

_____

_____

_____

57

How has your understanding and the meaning of success and happiness evolved over time?

_____

_____

_____

_____

_____

58

How do you plan to maintain an optimistic mindset and attitude as you face challenges in retirement?

_____

_____

_____

_____

_____

59

What are some specific things you would like to do "just with family" in retirement?

_____

_____

_____

_____

_____

60

What are some specific things you would like to do "just with friends" in retirement?

_____

_____

_____

_____

The Survey Says...

According to research from the Retirement Coaches Association:

Retirees report that the two key services that they wished they had access to before retiring were:
1) Finding purpose or direction
2) Staying relevant and savvy

90% of retirees feel that financial professionals should help them plan for the non-financial side of retirement... and 86% of retirees feel human resource professionals should help with non-financial planning as well.

76% of retirees have seen someone struggle with the transition.

43% of retirees reported that adjusting to retirement was harder than expected while 45% said adjusting took longer than expected. (4)

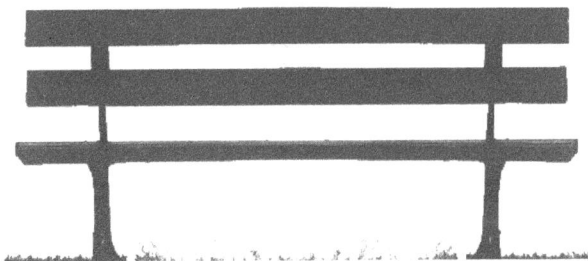

Section 5: Foundations

Questions: 61-74

69

61

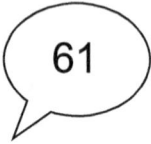

Where is your happy place and what role will it play in your retirement?

_____

_____

_____

_____

_____

62

How might your definition of home or primary residence change in retirement?

_____

_____

_____

_____

_____

63

Which aspirations or life long dreams do you want to pursue in retirement like... purchasing an RV... additional education... starting a business... travel, mission trips?

_____

_____

_____

_____

_____

64

What are your current thoughts, feelings, or plans about volunteering in retirement?

_____

_____

_____

_____

_____

65

What will be similar or different
about your physical activity and
nutritional habits in retirement?

_____

_____

_____

_____

_____

66

What makes you feel truly connected with someone?

_____

_____

_____

_____

_____

67

How would relocating or spending
several months in a different
location each year impact
your family responsibilities
and friendships?

_____

_____

_____

_____

_____

What are some healthy boundaries a new retiree may want to consider with an aging parent?

_____

_____

_____

_____

_____

69

What are some healthy boundaries a new retiree may want to consider with adult children?

_____

_____

_____

_____

_____

70

A friend is struggling to make a
retirement decision. What would
you suggest or share with them to
help them gain some clarity?

_____

_____

_____

_____

_____

What suggestions, ideas, and / or encouragements would you offer a friend who is being forced to retire a few years ahead of their originally planned exit?

_____

_____

_____

_____

_____

72

What advice do you have for a friend who is struggling to balance caring for their aging parents and spending time with their grandkids in two different locations?

_____

_____

_____

_____

_____

73

A friend's doctor is recommending they move to a different climate for preventive health reasons, but it would mean downsizing and leaving both family and friends. What suggestions do you have for them?

_____

_____

_____

_____

_____

74

Would you rather: work full time for two more years before retirement or pivot to part-time work for less pay and fewer benefits for five years before retirement? Why?

_____

_____

_____

_____

_____

The Wrong Top 10 List

Many people don't realize that retirement is one of the top 10 most stressful life events… and that 20 of the 43 other stressful events on the list can intersect directly with the retirement transition.

It's called the Holmes / Rahe Stress Scale and it was created by two psychiatrists, Thomas Holmes and Richard Rahe. Together, they surveyed 5,000 medical patients and found 43 life events that played a role in making the participants physically ill. They labeled each of these events as a Life Change Unit (LCU) and gave each one a "weight" on the scale.

Some other retirement related events on the list include a change in financial state, residential change, medical diagnosis, and the loss of a family member. (5)

Section 6: Legacy

Questions: 75-86

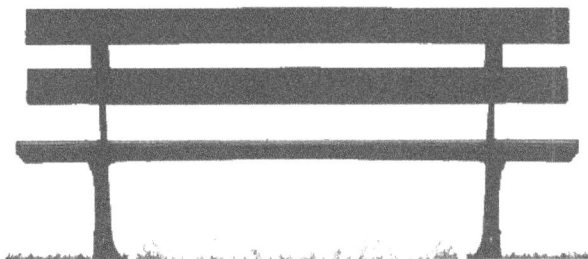

75

If you could only pass on one piece of wisdom to family and friends, what would it be?

_____

_____

_____

_____

_____

76

We all know that people are living
longer, so what does that increased
longevity mean to you?

_____

_____

_____

_____

_____

77

If "health-span" represents the number of years you will be in good health during retirement, what plans, goals, or dreams should <u>not</u> be delayed?

_____

_____

_____

_____

_____

78

When it comes to the giving of your time, energy, or resources, what are the specific organizations, groups, or causes that resonate the most with you?

_____

_____

_____

_____

_____

79

What does legacy mean to you
and what do you hope to pass
on besides money?

_____

_____

_____

_____

_____

80

What is your definition of a retirement well-lived?

_____

_____

_____

_____

81

What is something you would like to be known and remembered for?

_____

_____

_____

_____

_____

82

What steps can you take during retirement to make a lasting impact on family, friends and community?

A friend inherits a substantial amount of money but isn't sure how to share it with family, friends, or charities. What advice or ideas do you have for them?

_____

_____

_____

_____

_____

84

Which people in your life do you feel have been most influential in shaping your life and the legacy you'll leave behind?

_____

_____

_____

_____

_____

85

What are some of the things you are most grateful for as you reflect on your life leading up to retirement?

_____

_____

_____

_____

_____

How might your definition of legacy evolve or change over time and as you get older?

_____

_____

_____

_____

_____

Motivational Retirement Quotes

Success Is A Test
"A successful retirement isn't one without problems, but rather one in which you learn to overcome them."

You First, Money Second
"Running out of money pales in comparison to running out of family, friends, good health, & time."

Wisdom With Wealth:
"Transferring both wisdom and wealth is important because wealth doesn't create wisdom, however, wisdom can be used to maintain, build, and share wealth."

Retirement Isn't A Feeling
"You can't feel your way to and through retirement! So don't rely on how it may make you feel but rather on what you're going to do and the impact you want to have on others." (6)

Section 7: Couples

Questions: 87-98

87

What do you think are the biggest challenges for couples heading into retirement?

_____

_____

_____

_____

_____

88

What are the pros and cons for couples who retire at the same time or at different times?

_____

_____

_____

_____

89

Why should couples have individual friends outside of the couples they know and usually see together?

_____

_____

_____

_____

_____

What is the right mix of time that couples should plan or consider spending with 1) each other 2) time alone 3) family 4) friends?

_____

_____

_____

_____

_____

91

How might the expectations around traditional mealtimes including meal planning, preparations, and how often a couple may eat alone or together change in retirement?

_____

_____

_____

_____

_____

92

How might bedtime and morning routines for couples remain the same or be different in retirement?

_____

_____

_____

_____

93

How might household roles and responsibilities change or need to be adjusted in retirement?

_____

_____

_____

_____

_____

94

What are a few things that couples may need to sacrifice in order to make each other's time in retirement the best it can be?

_____

_____

_____

_____

_____

What are some ways that couples can respect and support each other's personal goals and build shared goals to pursue together in retirement?

_____

_____

_____

_____

_____

How can couples deal with and work through one partner or spouse having very clear direction and purpose but the other is feeling stuck and unsure of what's next?

_____

_____

_____

_____

_____

What steps can and should couples take to stay healthy and active before and throughout retirement?

_____

_____

_____

_____

_____

98

What health issues might affect
a couples retirement timeline or
lifestyle and how can they prepare
to support each other if one of them
experiences health decline?

_____

_____

_____

_____

Quotes For We-tirement

"I married you for better or for worse, but not for lunch every day in retirement."

"Married life in retirement: Twice as much spouse with half the pay."

"Honey, I'm home forever!"

"Beware: There's a retired spouse running lose in the house!"

"We finally decided to spend the kids inheritance. Unfortunately, they insisted on coming with us!"

"I thought I was retired, but now I work for my spouse!"

"A newly retired partner can sometimes be the full-time job of the other spouse."
(7)

Section 8: Wrap Up

Questions: 99-101

99

What themes or ideas continued to come up throughout the questions?

_____

_____

_____

_____

_____

100

What did you uncover, rediscover, and learn about yourself (and or others if you used it in a group)?

_____

_____

_____

_____

_____

101

If you had to tell a family member, friend, or colleague about this book, how would you describe it and what would you say is your favorite section and question?

_____

_____

_____

_____

_____

Other Resources From The RCA

The Retirement Challenge:
A Non-financial Guide From
Top Retirement Experts

Out Of The Box Retirement:
Creative Ideas, Role Models,
and New Possibilities

Rightsourcing Retirement:
Best Practices For Employers
And Employees

The Retirement Collective:
Shared Wisdom From Top
Retirement Coaches

The Next Chapter Is Yours!
Real Stories & Bold Moves
For Your Retirement

*Thriving Throughout Your
Retirement Transition*

The Fine Print Of Retirement

Retirement Coaches Association

The RCA is a group of dedicated professionals who are committed to helping people thrive in this next phase of life! Our goal is to not only help you see and experience retirement in a truly different and more meaningful light but also to help you:

- Formulate a vision for your future.
- Unlock & expand your potential.
- Reinforce and maximize you strengths.
- Formulate a plan to keep you relevant, connected, and active.
- Provide encouragement and objective feedback.
- Develop balance in your life now and in the future.
- Support your efforts and provide you with increased confidence.

- Brainstorm strategies and ideas to accomplish your goals.
- Uncover and assist in developing your unique abilities.
- Inspire you toward continuous improvement and unparalleled results.

To find a coach near you or to learn more about the organization and our mission to modernize retirement planning, please visit:

RetirementCoachesAssociation.org.

Sources

(1) Did You Know, Pg., 13
   Certified Retirement Coach
   Designation manual, Robert Laura

(2) Anonymous Retirement Plan Pg., 32
   Snopes.com This is a fictional story

(5) Retirement Humor, Pg., 83
   Google AI web search

(4) Survey Say Pg., 67
   Great Retirement Disconnect
   Retirement Coaches Association

(5) The Wrong Top 10 List., Pg.55
   Holmes Rahe Scale Wikipedia

(6) Motivational Quotes, Pg., 97
   Quotes from Robert Laura, RCA
   Founder

(7) Quotes For We-tirement, Pg., 117
   Google AI web search